Off The Cuffs

A Collection of Essays by Master No One

To my beloved Feisty Geisty, thank you for loving me until I was me again.

TABLE OF CONTENTS

Preface/Introduction

Who are you?

Three simple words that can have an infinite possibility of answers. However, despite the simplicity of this short text, I begin it with this complicated question.

If you are reading these words, I can deduce that you are curious, intelligent, and strive to learn and understand all the many things of the world that are as of yet, ungraspable. I can also deduce that there is a growing urge inside of you for something dark and passionate, and you believe the answers may lie within these modest writings of a humble master.

Thank you for placing such faith in me. However, before we embark on such a hazardous journey of the self, I must warn you; I cannot tell you the answers, I can only pose to you the correct questions.

Of course, that leads us to who am I?

I will not point out the paradox of you asking a masked man who he is, but I will tell you what I can.

My scene name is Master No One, a name that was gifted to me by a close friend. Many of us adopt pseudonyms when entering the Fetish scene or local BDSM community because of fear of reprisal for our sexual interests, but unfortunately, the cloak of anonymity can give license to our worst character vices, rather than allowing us to exhibit our better virtues, but that can be discussed later.

I am a male in my early thirties, with over 10 years of experience in the Southern California BDSM scene. I find comfort in being a sado-masochistic Dominant, and will occasionally switch in private with my partner if the chemistry is right. My favorite fetishes are latex clothing, leather & chain bondage, inflicting consensually sadistic pain, and mind-fuckery.

I am a cis-gendered male, white-ish, jew-ish, and bipolar-ish.

I am heterosexual, and with your permission, I believe that the essays collected within will help any Kinkster, of any orientation or position on the gender spectrum.

My exploits are many, and while I believe it is ungentlemanly to kiss and tell, I will tell you that I have experienced: spanking women in public; Jacuzzi sex; public sex; having a beautiful woman do nude clerical work for me; a Scientologist threatening to kill me; rocking out with cool men in Mohawks; and discovering a large naked man sitting on a public Hollywood street corner; and that was just one particular weekend.

Part of the reason I was able to experience all this is because for a brief time, I ran the Los Angeles kink education and performance group, Fetish Noir. During my administration, we organized three BDSM town hall panels (Performance and Kink, Kink in Art, and Ethics in BDSM Porn), we created a revolutionary mentor program bringing together newbies and experienced players, we held our own parties at the Los Angeles BDSM club, Threshold, forged partnerships to bring in Fetish Noir Party Mentors for Los Angeles Fetish clubs (including Fetish Nation, Bondage Ball, Erotic City at L.A. Pride, Underworld, and Bar Sinister), received membership in the Los Angeles Leather Coalition by a unanimous vote, raised hundreds of dollars for Operation Homefront to benefit our troops, and most importantly, because of our organization, people's lives were literally and directly saved.

Many considered me a Master, which connotes power; but as Martin Luther King said, "I am not interested in power for power's sake, but... in power that is moral, that is right, and that is good." In the BDSM scene (and in life), power is either given with trust, or taken by force; the former is an exercise in erotically informed consent, the latter is a felony. I did not seek the title of Master, but I came to embrace it because it was a title that showed I was trusted by my lovers, my friends, and my community, and because of my interactions in the community, it helped me become a better person.

I call myself a Master, and while you, gentle reader, may only see me as some foolish vice-ridden pervert whose friends are porn stars and dominatrices, I know about art, love, brotherhood, and the grandeur of the universe, if only because I long for it with every fiber of my being.

So, I pose our introductory question again: Who are you?

The following is a collection of essays I wrote over the four years I was immersed in the Los Angeles BDSM scene. Over that time, I learned much about myself, and I hope that they will help you reflect on your own journey. So, together, let us discover the treasure that lies in the dark corners of your uncharted soul.

The Night No One Was Born

A sadist cannot be a sadist without a consenting masochistic partner. A dominant cannot be a dominant without a submissive... Well, they can, it would just be weird and kind of creepy. As a Dominant, we must dance our dance with many partners over our lives, but we must take care to be good dance partners, or we will have no one to dance with. They knew this when they invented Tango dancing in the brothels of Buenos Aires, and even 2,000 years ago, when Jesus told the story of the Good Samaritan. And so we must ask ourselves: Do we take care of our dance partners? Do we protect our partners? Do we provide something of value to our partners? And most importantly, do we take responsibility for how our actions affect the lives and experiences of those around us?

Sweat dripped down her arms and lips as she hung there, blindfolded, hands cuffed to a cable in the center of the room like a meat hook hangs an innocent calf. I paced around her, gazing at my captive prey, ready to pounce.

Making sure the sleazebags and gropers stayed away, I did the best I could to intimidate them with all 5'8" of me, but I refused to let them distract me from my conquest. I kept her guessing, a brush of the hand here, a whisper in the ear there, never letting her know where I would land next, or with what weapon.

I wanted her scared.

I wanted her waiting in anticipation, not knowing what was coming, and too confused to guess.

The ice dripping down from inside her bra, and the heat from her flogged back sent her sensations for a tailspin, and after two hours of pleasure and pain radiating through every muscle, bone, and nerve ending in her body, she couldn't take any more. Her body buckled under the pressure, going limp.

I guided her to the floor, slipping a pillow under her sore ass for good measure, and as she sipped her water and looked up into my eyes, she said, "My God, I've never cum so many times in my life."

That was the night I met Lasher, that was the night I knew what I had become, and I loved it.

The Growing Toy Bag

Any great task requires tools. Whether it be as simple as a walking stick, or as complicated as an ICBM missile, we must have the tools to use. However, having the tools is one thing, but knowing how to use them can be another. How do we prepare? And are we prepared to use these tools?

Below is a list of items for a proper toy bag, compiled from Jack Rinella's "The Master's Manual" with a few notes of my own. I should also add a small note beforehand, that having a proper toy bag is different for everyone, based on his or her own skills and preferences. The below should serve as a general guide.

Toy bags can get very expensive, so ideally, you should go in the following order: SAFETY ITEMS FIRST; then CHEAP ITEMS second; and then MORE EXPENSIVE ITEMS SHOULD FOLLOW AS YOU LEARN HOW TO PROPERLY USE THEM.

How will you know if you know how to properly use them? Try them on yourself first. ALWAYS TRY THEM ON YOURSELF FIRST. Or if you can, have someone else try them on you.

You can start out with a smaller sized bag, realizing you'll upgrade as your skillset improves. For the first two years I was in the scene, my toy bag was a compact Polaroid camera bag, and I had to choose which toys I was going to bring to the club. Having to pick and choose which toys I could bring to an event seemed like a hindrance at first, but it also forced me to think about what I wanted to do that night, and what activities I was interested in. As the French painter, Georges Braque, said, "It is the limitation of means that determines style, gives rise to new forms and makes creativity possible."

Also, all of these things can be found on the Internet if you don't like the sources listed.

THE PROPER TOY BAG (ala Jack Rinella, author of "The Master's Manual")

---SAFETY ITEMS---

• EMT safety scissors (preferably with a bright colored handle for easy locating in the dark) (medical supply stores, some 99¢ stores, some convenient stores, the internet)

• ACE Bandage (for wounds or improvised blindfold) (most Rite Aids or CVS', some 99¢ stores)

• Mini First Aid Kit (most Rite Aids or CVS')

• Bag/Box of Latex Gloves (Nitrile gloves are equally good, or better, in case someone has a latex allergy)(Rite Aid, CVS, 99¢ stores)

• Small amount of soap or bleach (99¢ stores)

• Plenty of large Ziploc bags to keep your toys separate from one another and clean. (Ralphs, 99¢ stores)

• Condoms (Rite Aid or CVS)

• A nondescript bag (gym bag, rolling luggage, or art supply kit)

• Printed out copies of a Yes/No/Maybe List and a list of negotiation questions for the Dom to ask the sub

---CHEAP ITEMS---

• Rubber Bands (99¢ stores)

• Plastic Wrap and/or duct tape (99¢ stores)

• Twist-ties (good for quick restraining through those small loop holes) (99¢ stores)

• Lubricant (stored in Ziploc for leakage protection) (Rite Aid or CVS)

- Shoe laces (99¢ stores)

- A Wooden or Leather paddle (99¢ stores, look under cutting boards)

- Hairbrush (99¢ stores)

- Ben Gay (for loosening up the anus) (Rite Aid or CVS)

- Candles, preferably soft wax-in-glass candles (also known as Jesus candles) since they burn at a cooler temperature. Remember, the harder the wax, and the darker the wax, the hotter it will burn your partner. (99¢ stores)

- Lighter/Matches (remember, lighter fluid will evaporate if you leave your toy bag in the sun or a hot car) (99¢ stores)

- Blindfold (99¢ stores)

- Clothespins (Though you can get wooden clothespins at 99¢ stores, these are usually very flimsy and break easily, so it's best to get the plastic ones which are tougher from a Target or K-mart)

- A blanket or cloth (for aftercare) (Target)

- Aloe and/or massage oils (for Aftercare) (Target)

---MORE SKILLED AND/OR EXPENSIVE ITEMS---

- Dog choke chain (any pet store)

- Dog leash (any pet store)

- Dog collar (any pet store)

- Fishing Weights (most sports and tackle shops)

- Nylon Fishing Line (most sports and tackle shops)

- Hanging Hooks, Carabineers, and other fastening devices (Home Depot)

- Leather Belt

- Buggy Whip (Equestrian shop)

- Riding Crop (Equestrian shops or sex shops)

- Small locks (always double check the key that opens it before you use it on someone... some day I'll tell you about a really funny story when I was in Lower Manhattan) (Home Depot)

- Rope (preferably hemp) (internet)

- Handcuffs (sex shops)

- Leather Wrist and Ankle Restraints (sex shops)

- Nipple clamps (with rubber shields) (sex shops)

- Leather Thongs (sex shops)

- Ball stretchers (sex shops)

- Leather hood (lace backing is better because it's more adjustable) (sex shop)

- Cat of Nine Tails or Flogger (sex shop)

- Dildo(s) and or butt plug(s) (varying in size) (sex shops, although if anyone can find one at a 99¢ store, post a pic and I'll buy you dinner)

- Whip (professional leather craftsman only, and make sure you know how to use it before you buy it, since these can range in the hundreds)

Sex Logistics Checklist

Let us take a moment to reflect on our adventures. The humorous essay below is a To Do List parody. However, I included it because behind every joke is a silver lining of truth. As we embark on this journey, we may dance with many different partners over many different times in our lives, and we must consider as we dance, what is the end pleasurable experience? What do we want? What does our partner want? Can we negotiate to get what we both want?

Like the boy scouts, it's good to be prepared for any possible option. So, for everyone's benefit, I have comprised a list of items that EVERY kinkster should have nearby. This can be kept in the special 'sex drawer', or in the 'sex closet'. My slave and I choose to keep these nearby in the special 'sex credenza'.

- Condoms

- Nitrile Gloves

- Lube

- Towel

- Hitachi

- Aftercare Blanket

- Water Bottle(s) (2 or more depending on number of participants)

- Chocolate

- Paper Towels

- Alcohol (Cleaning Purposes)

- Dirty Talk Dictionary

- Pads/Tampons

- Blood Pressure Medication

- Emergency Sandwich
- Talcum Powder
- Romantic Candles
- Home Enema Kit
- Kneepads
- Helmet

The 10 Kink Commandments

A wise man once said, 'If you don't stick to your values when they're being tested, they're not values: they're hobbies.' That was Jon Stewart, former anchor of the Daily Show, who at times, served as America's own Jiminy Cricket. As we go down this path, we will come upon people and events that challenge our beliefs and us. Sometimes we need to be challenged, but it's important to know before setting off, what do you stand for?

1. All activity must be safe (we do not cause true harm), sane (we only engage in activity when we are clear of mind), and consensual.

2. One must always be respectful of your partner's safe word (red/yellow/green) and their hard limits.

3. We only enter into activities after we have gained trust, education, and an open mind.

4. Always be polite and ask questions.

5. Do not touch anyone else's equipment without permission.

6. We always must be clean, hygienic, and mindful of our own equipment.

7. We will always be mindful of aftercare.

8. We do not engage in humiliating and degrading scenes for solely our own amusement.

9. We always protect one another's anonymity from the harsh eyes of the vanilla world.

10. And most importantly, don't forget to have a good time.

There's No Money In Kink

For a long time now, people have been told the mantra, 'If you can make money doing what you love, you'll never work a day in your life.' However, if you do what you love for a living, you'll probably wind up loving it a little bit less. Why would I want to bring up this topic in a book about BDSM? Well, lots of people love sex! Because of this, many people think they can turn their newfound discovery of BDSM into a lucrative career, complete with horny, naked (and Gothy) co-eds. Many people jump at the opportunity to pursue such endeavors. However, can we separate our job and what we love as separate parts of our holistic identity? Or do we feel the need to identify our sexuality as the whole of our beings? Are we financially stable enough to embark on this road?

I got into a very passionate conversation at a party tonight with someone about Kink and the community, and we both came to the same conclusion.

There's no money in Kink.

Seriously, there's no money in kink! If you look at all the different ways of monetizing BDSM, it's just not practically feasible.

There's a romantic aspect to the idea of making money by doing what you love. The glamour of the shiny clothing, the sexy toys, and the money are hard to resist. After having befriended and even dated some of the most influential and well-known people in the L.A. Fetish Community, I have talked with them, and been invited into their homes, and I can tell you this; There Is No Money In The L.A. BDSM Scene.

I've known club promoters and pornographers, sex toy makers and strippers, fetish photographers and models, and every single one of them uses their income from the BDSM scene as a small supplement to an already existing form of vanilla income. There's no way to maintain a stable income from the BDSM world, let alone build a luxurious fortune. The only people who have really made it work, are people that all, coincidentally, own their own venues, and I can count those individuals on a single hand.

Now don't get me wrong, this lifestyle is fun (it sure beats the hell out of stamp collecting), but it's recreational, pure and simple.

Let's go down the list of job opportunities in the scene and see how profitable they are.

Dungeon Monitor – Strictly a volunteer position. It's a noble and important position, but you do it because you want to give back to the community, not because you want something out of it.

Organizer - A lot of times, this is a truly selfless act. Organizing a BDSM event outside of the traditional dungeon party is important. Organizers help breathe new life into this community, by bringing new ideas and aesthetics to our world of parties and events. Without a foundation of volunteers to organize events and build into them the values of sex-positivity, open-mindedness, consent and safety, the scene would not be what it is. People like SubMissAnn who organized the Southern California Fox Hunt, or Mistress Matilda who organized the Trevor Project class for Fetish Noir. These people are important, and can give real character to a local community by putting their own stamp on it, and deserve all the credit they get.

Pro-Domme/Sub – There's a certain amount of glamour about such a position because of how sexy it is. The little-known fact about going pro is that you only get a couple of clients a week, and that number can go down in a poor economy. You basically make less money than if you were working a 9 to 5 job at Starbucks, and have less stability.

Porn Director/Producer - Porn director Billy Watson wrote, "Like most business, porn's struggling. Unlike most, porn's business model is competing against something fierce and mighty. To really complicate things, it's a business model has changed radically in the last five years... and no one likes change." He goes on to say, "Porn Valley is drying up, and fast. People are freaking out. Agencies are closing. More than 90% of the jobs are being booked by less than 10% of the companies. Rates are dropping. No one's sure when it'll come back — if it ever does." One noted male porn star has commented, "this business has bankrupted me. Fuck porn!" Citations can be found in http://www.ishootporn.com/?p=3905

Porn Actor/Actress - This job suffers from the same economic problems a Pro-Domme does, lack of reliability. It's the same problem that any actor in Los Angeles has: you have long droughts of unemployment, and you get overworked and underpaid when you are employed. Also, according to Chico Wang, noted porn director, "I would say 90% of the girls in the industry hate what they do and fuck only for money... I would also say that 99% of the girls in the industry have serious issues such as but not limited to previous bouts with rape, incest, molestation, drug abuse, pimp boyfriends, etc." http://www.ishootporn.com/?p=126

Club Performer - The vast number of club performers in the L.A. BDSM scene don't make any money. They are allowed free entry to parties, but that's it. When I first heard this, I thought it was a load of crap too, but it turns out to be true. Plus, they have the pressure of getting a certain quota of people in on their list. The only performers I've ever seen get paid were a few women at the larger events such as Bondage Ball and L.A. Kink Ball.

Club Promoter - If you're promoting a BDSM club, you get a small promotional fee (and by small I mean not even enough to pay your monthly rent) and then a percentage of the door after the club breaks even which can be manipulated through funny math.

Toy Maker - There's one logistical problem that every toy maker faces. No matter how beautiful or unique your design is, you can't mass-produce your product. These are handmade pieces of craftsmanship with very expensive materials that take numerous man-hours. As a result, many toy makers sell their goods at a high price, but make minimal profit.

Venue Owner - This is truly the only position that can be profitable in the scene. If you compare it to a proper business model, you can look at it as a real estate investment, and as such, you can sell space, and reinvest into the property. However, in any marketplace, there's a certain cap on the market, and you can't spread the customers too thin.

In addition, in order to move forward with these business endeavors, they still have to follow the rules of entrepreneurship and economics: supply and demand; finding customers; managing employees; etc. As John Nash explained in Game Theory, the ideal strategy is the strategy that is good for the individual, and the group.

That Person You Love Is Quietly Destroying You
OR: How To Spot An Emotionally Manipulative Narcissist

As we meet new dance partners and make new lifelong friends, we must ask ourselves questions about them, and about ourselves. Are we emotionally stable for this endeavor? Are we aware of the emotional stability of others?

I was attending a book talk a few months ago at a local Borders, for Dr. Drew's newest book <u>The Mirror Effect: How Celebrity Narcissism Is Seducing America</u>. Now, I knew little about narcissism, and had lost my love of Dr. Drew when I realized how anti-kink he was, but there was nothing good on TV that night, so I figured, what the hell.

He had co-written the book with another doctor from USC (GO TROJANS!) and it was fun seeing the two interact, watching how he kept making fun of Dr. Drew for being a Hollywood doctor, and watching Dr. Drew get flustered every time he mentioned it.

They also discussed how the narcissist is, despite common misconceptions, not in love with themselves. Narcissists are in fact deeply insecure people, who feel compelled to put the people around them down in order to build themselves up and feel validated. For some reason, this struck a chord with me, so I tried to read the book.

I say 'tried' because I am a notoriously slow reader. I have books from 2001 that I still haven't gotten around to. It's one of my many flaws. So rather than buying it, I read as much of it as I could in Borders, and went home to read everything I could find on the subject online.

I realized something. My parents were textbook narcissists. My Dad was someone who constantly put my sisters and I down, telling me things like I wasn't smart enough to be a garbage man, and that I never used common sense. My Mom was desperately emotionally clingy and needy, and constantly needed emotional validation.

Since then, I've fallen into a string of similar relationships with narcissists: romantic relationships; business relationships; community-based relationships; etc.

It's easy to spot a narcissist once you identify the pattern.

The narcissist is often excited to meet you and always charming. However, they have a unique charm, a shallow charm that rather than being engaged with you, is someone who has that schmoozy attitude of "always glad to see you."

When you start to get to know them, and ask questions like "What do you do for fun?" or "What do you do for a living?" They will "burst with joy to share how incredible they are; and every thing that they have achieved. ([It's normal to] mention some things that [you're] proud of; but [most people] have to think it through a bit.) [Narcissists] can't stop talking about themselves and how great they are." (Associated Content)

This is part of a tactic to lure you in: sparking your interests, and attracting you to them so that they can use you for their own motives. In my own personal experiences, the more destructive narcissists will lure you in with a great new idea or project that they are working on. The project is one of a kind and revolutionary, and of course the kind of project that everyone will want to work on, but you are getting this special opportunity to work with them and get in on the ground floor.

They are happy to see you because they need to lure you in, so they will always be charming towards you as long as there is the potential that they can use you. Remember, abuse is a two-person tango, and they cannot fulfill their own personal needs unless you take the bait.

A good hint that you are dealing with a narcissist is how they will speak of others. Will they trash talk their peers, or supposed friends?

They will phrase their words very carefully, in a way that makes you and the narcissist appear as the good guys, and that you are fighting against the others (the scapegoats) as the bad guys. The more skilled narcissists will craft a narrative, and use your passionate interests as the institution or the values that the scapegoat is trying to destroy.

Some will use the idea of a conspiracy theory. Some will say, "They are spearheading a witch hunt." While others will say, "They've turned into something disgusting and unkind." This is not a scapegoat tactic; these are their own legitimate thoughts. Unfortunately, these are thoughts fueled by paranoia. This kind of revisionist fantasy is common, and something that will turn on you.

Unfortunately, this is for the purpose of manipulation... manipulation of YOU. His goal is for you to eventually think, "Any time he tells you he's happy for you and he encourages you to do something, he'll REALLY mean it, with YOU. He won't create a revisionist fantasy of your past so that he can insist you did things to hurt him as a justification for his cruelty to you. He won't secretly resent you for not devoting all your time to him." (Heartless)

Once they feel they have gained your confidence, they begin to slowly show their true colors, the abusive side. One doctor said, "Even though I have a Master's in psychology, it did not help me identify and deal with people who are severely narcissistic. The cues, the verbal abuse and emotional abuse, and the manipulation, can be subtle and insidious; our sense of self erodes over time as the narcissist slowly undermines us." (NSR) This portion of the relationship could last a while, because the whole point of this is for the narcissist to use you like a crutch.

The goal of this is to make you think, "He won't get mopey and upset because you get more attention than he does at social functions. He won't resent you for your charisma. Just because he did that before doesn't mean he's going to do it again with YOU. As long as you make sure HE is the center of attention, and he's getting his ego stroked, he probably won't get nasty with you... Right? It couldn't be that he is a bottomless pit, and that you can NEVER give him enough attention. Not the man YOU know. Not with YOU. You're special." (Heartless) By the way, the majority of these quotes focus on the Narcissist as a man, but the Narcissist can be any gender. Narcissism knows no bounds, and it manifests in every role and age.

Eventually there will be a dramatic turn in the relationship. This turn will stem from the reason that they chose to use you in the first place, and the point that you stop being of value to them. Whether you no longer sexually fulfill them, emotionally validate them, financially support them, you are perceived as a threat to their power and popularity, you are unruly and disobedient, or maybe they're just plain bored with you, they eventually turn on you and throw you under the bus. "In other words: they use people, generally to make them look good and will not give rejecting you a second thought; if you stop providing them with an Ego stroke. Generally you cannot get them to apologize...I mean ever. No kidding here." (Associated Content)

They will begin by throwing you under the bus to their friends, saying that you're not worth their time, or you are a deeply flawed human being. Eventually, they will get bolder and bolder, trash talking and rumormongering you to your circle of mutual friends. Sometimes they'll lie and say things like "he plays when he drinks" or "he's unsafe with a knife" and if you stick around for long enough, they'll eventually use direct verbal abuse. They don't do this because they want to. They do it because they need to in order to feel comfortable with themselves.

This is an unhealthy form of BDSM to say the least. But, you don't have to get stuck with one. Here are some ways to spot (and avoid) someone who could be potentially destructive to your psyche.

- Do they go out of their way to put down others?

- Do they encourage you to make self-destructive decisions?

- Do they have strong opinions about most things and seem to get too "into" it, and remind you of a preacher, or a sailor depending on their habits towards cussing?

- When they talk about their last relationships, do they launch into a tirade about how much they hate them?

- When you ask them what they want, do they only focus on material things that they want to get personally, and avoid bringing up what they can offer you?

- Is this person a namedropper?

- Are they preoccupied with ideas of unlimited success, power, brilliance, beauty, or ideal love, and never do anything to achieve them?

It may seem harsh to judge people in this way, especially someone who may appear charming, friendly, and even a prominent figure in the community, but it is absolutely necessary in order to protect ourselves. Just as we take precautions when meeting someone new for fear of physical harm, we must also take precautions for fear of mental & emotional harm.

If I may quote a leader of the L.A. Kink community, *I know it's painfully popular to say things like, "Don't judge people". Well, I assert that not judging people or events is not only absurd, it's impossible to not judge people and be able to make informed choices. Of course we need to make value judgments. Without making some judgments about the people and events we encounter would leave us hopelessly incapable of making even the simplest of choices. If someone is telling me about a concern they have, I'm judging their words and therefore them very carefully. So let's agree that the "not judging people" statement doesn't mean "Don't make critical analysis decisions about information and people" but it means, "When you come across someone who does something that doesn't necessarily appeal to you but is not harming people and it's their own business, don't condemn them for it." I know, it's longer and doesn't have the same marketable pizzazz as "Don't judge people!" but it's really what is meant by the aphorism. To summarize: We judge, and that's a wise and healthy thing to do. It's self-righteous and fatuous condemnation that is inappropriate, not judgment.* - Master George

For more information, check out the The Narcissistic Vampire Checklist or The DSM-IV Diagnostic Criteria for Narcissistic Personality Disorder

Burnout (Thoughts After 13 Months of Reflection)

After running the performance and education group Fetish Noir for a year, and helping run another BDSM group prior to that, I was overwhelmed. I had spent eighteen months pushing myself to the brink, going to two or three parties a week, promoting events, and having sex and play so frequently that it lost it's appeal. I eventually chose to quit the public scene, because I had burnt the candle so brightly that it blew out. I had to recharge my batteries. After thirteen months of break from the scene, I posted this essay, explaining my reasons. Part of me hoped that my example could prevent other people from making the same mistake, and another part of me wanted to articulate a lot of frustrations that I had kept bottled in. So, with this last essay, I ask you, when is it too much for you? What is the point for you of diminishing returns?

I got this question one too many times, and felt the need to explain it more elaborately. I wrote this about six months ago and have been sitting on it. I was urged to post it by a close friend.

Let me be up front, there were several reasons I quit the scene, and they were all personal. I can't point to one objective reason and say, 'I left the scene because of the drama about this person or that club.' I can't say that it was something that could be fixed. It was a complicated mesh of issues that layered on top of one another.

I will say this, I didn't quit because I'm not kinky, I am still very much kinky. I didn't quit because I don't like hanging out with kinky people. I love hanging out with kinky people.

I quit the PUBLIC scene because of the following reasons:

1. I got cheated on too many times. The majority of the relationships I've had in the scene have ended with me getting cheated on. I'm monogamous. I like being monogamous. I like the emotional depth of a loving relationship that I didn't get when I tried being Poly. When my girlfriends cheated on me, it was

heartbreaking, and I was sick and tired of going through that. What's the point of being a Master, if you can't stop the woman you love from sleeping with someone else?

2. The most important reason was I had a personal realization. My sexuality is an important part of my identity, but it's not the ONLY part of my identity. Yes, I'm kinky, but I'm also a horseback rider. I'm also into swing dancing, and comedy clubs, and physics, and movies, and politics. I am more complex than an anonymous list of fetishes could show. But in the scene, those lists of fetishes are the first thing, and sometimes the only thing that people care about, and that emphasis by other people changes where we put our own energies and time management. It teaches us to value people sexually, and just in terms of what they could give us, rather than what we can share. If you've tried to start a relationship with someone just based on your common fetishes, you know already that it can be awkward, uncomfortable, and a one-dimensional interaction. A friend from the LALC said it best, 'Nowadays, people can go onto FetLife or Recon, and look up a list of their fetishes like a checklist, and just hook up and get whatever they want without ever having a real connection with someone.' While the on demand hookup can be exciting, I do not want my kink to absorb my entire life.

3. Time. Most people have to work 40 hours a week (or go to school and work). Even if you don't take a leadership position in the scene like I did with Fetish Noir, let's look at the breakdown. You go to one club night a week. That's 1 or 2 hours to get dressed. There's travel time. There's the time you spend at the actual club. Then the after-club activities: either you go home and stay up late playing/fucking, or you go to Denny's and stay up 'til 4 or 5 am with your friends. Then the next day you wake up late, and you have to readjust your sleep schedule for work, which could take a night or two. To make matters worse, when one takes on leadership and organizing, such as I did working Fetish Noir as a second job, it can be frustrating to be putting in all this work, and not able to get paid, or put it on my resume. I

wouldn't have changed the experience for anything, but it was still frustrating.

4. Oversaturation. After going to multiple play parties a week for over a year, I just got tired of it. I got to a point where I just couldn't handle going to another play party ever again, and I still feel that way. There's so much to be enjoyed outside of a dungeon party, and being oversaturated loses a lot of perspective.

5. I am seriously uncomfortable with how the deceptive and abusive sex industries are intertwined with this community. I've said this before, and I'll say it again, I have no concern for strict Christian, slut-shaming morality. I'm a Deist, and I believe God is at best, an absentee landlord. My main concerns are physical safety, mental health, and long-term upward mobility and when someone chooses to work in the sex trades, it hurts all three. I've dated sex workers, including Pro-Doms. When I hear about someone wanting to start working at a local dungeon or do videos in order to make extra money, I see it as someone who is exercising self-destructive tendencies. It's like looking at someone who drinks until they get drunk, and they are howling at the moon that they can stop any time they want to, even though they are vomiting in the street and feel like shit. And then, when bad things happen, they complain about being a victim, when they have put themselves in that situation in the first place. I eventually realized, you can't save every hooker with a heart of gold.

And everyone else doesn't want to be seen as judgmental, so they say, 'Way to go!' 'It's your body!' 'Girl power!' but then when the sex worker in question can't pay their rent, is suffering from problems due to stress and other issues, and has surrounded themselves with nefarious characters, we all bite our collective tongues.

6. Kinky sex got boring. My friend, Dorian, asked me, "I bet as head of Fetish Noir, you got a lot of pussy?" I'm not going to lie. Many women were more attracted to me because I was

seen as a leader in the community. I heard a woman say this once, "Power is to women, what cleavage is to men." Power is sexy (whether that power is real, or only misperceived), and yes, I had a lot of nights of wild sex. But, it got boring. Now, the women I slept with were amazing. They went to town! But sex without love, eventually gets boring. No matter how many toys you use, no matter how many techniques you learn, no matter how many people are watching, unless you have something of substance there, it's not really worth it. The expression is "spice it up" for a reason; it's spice, not a meal. In the movie, METALLICA SOME KIND OF MONSTER, one of the band members said, 'Every night, going out, getting high, passing out, it's the same, and it just got boring. Now I have a wife and kids, and I have no idea what's going to happen next. That's the exciting part!'

7. I've got bigger things to accomplish. I want to change the world. I want to fight for the underprivileged. I want to help end genocide. I want to increase education standards. I want to fight for a worldwide minimum wage. I want to build a Department of International Government Reconstruction. But I can't do that unless I get my priorities in order. Some naïve individuals may say I'm a traitor to my people for that, but we don't live in a perfect world, and sometimes in order to do the things we feel compelled to do, we have to make personal sacrifices to our time and leisure activities.

8. It's just not as important as everyone makes it, and we are not victims. I'll be honest, I've considered coming back to the scene, even running back as fast as my hairy legs will carry me. Call it what you want, nostalgia, boredom, loneliness, but every time I get the urge, something happens; a colleague dies, a tsunami hits, a friend needs my help, etc. Something happens that shocks me and shows me that there's more to life than this world of fantasy and club rats that we've created for ourselves. Some people want to create a BDSM pride day, similar to gay pride day, and that I think is an insult to gay people. We are not an oppressed minority, just a misunderstood one. We are not the

victim of any government organization or even a religious right movement (hell, most people in the religious right are kinky too). Everyone keeps crying, "We're victims, we're victims!" Who are we being victimized by? Nobody has shown me any concrete proof that we are, in fact, an oppressed group in this country. If anything, we are victims of poor organization from our own leaders, and the fact that we are a small niche section of society.

9. One of the biggest reasons is, I'm still not sure if lifestyle BDSM and the public scene as it exists today is entirely healthy. Yes, the public scene is better than people being repressed and afraid of their genitals. Yes, the public scene is better than wandering around on the Internet, and being potential prey for homicidal rapists. Yes, the public scene is better than couples not receiving any information at all, and accidentally killing each other with stupid dangerous play. BUT! We all come to the scene with our own individual brokenness, and there's nothing wrong with that. There's nothing wrong with saying, 'I'm OCD, or Depressed, or Bi-Polar, and I need medication in order to stabilize my thoughts and function.' There's nothing wrong with admitting that.

But, is there something wrong with saying, "Oh yeah, I was diagnosed that, but I'm fine. Now cut me!"?

Is there something wrong with someone turning down talk-therapy, and using a BDSM scene to recreate the rape, molestation, or trauma that was inflicted upon them?

Is there something wrong with putting all these people with emotional illnesses in the same space, and letting them feed off each other's energies, allowing their issues to grow like a petri dish?

Is there something wrong with hierarchical, closed-off, and isolated groups forming, which closely resemble a controlling and authoritarian cult?

I don't know. What do you think?

Some of these thoughts may have affected you because they challenged your preconceptions about the scene, and maybe even about yourself and why you're in it, and that's good. Self-reflection and change should be a central focus of our existence, for as Winston Churchill said, "To improve is to change; to be perfect is to change often."

Thank You

That is it my friend, we have reached the end of our time together.

If you enjoyed this collection of essays, then I humbly thank you for your time, and I hope I've given you plenty of things to think about.

Please leave a review on Amazon discussing what you enjoyed.

Now, I am not by any stretch of the imagination telling you to answer all of these questions before you proceed down this long and windy road. I say, go forth, and you will find the answers you need.

I will be publishing a more in-depth book discussing my experiences in the L.A. BDSM community entitled **No One Was Here; The True Story of Sex, Drugs, Murder, Fetish, and How One Man's World Collided With It All**. Subscribe to my Authors Page on Amazon, or my page on FetLife, to find out more details about me, and my upcoming works.

Thank you again, and I look forward to offering you more salacious insights very soon.